# WHAT IS A DICTATORSHIP?

SARAH B. BOYLE

 Crabtree Publishing Company

www.crabtreebooks.com

# Crabtree Publishing Company

www.crabtreebooks.com

**Produced and developed by Netscribes Inc.**

**Author:** Sarah B. Boyle
**Publishing plan research and development:**
   Sean Charlebois, Reagan Miller
   Crabtree Publishing Company
**Editors:** Valerie J. Weber, Lynn Peppas
**Proofreader:** Wendy Scavuzzo
**Art director:** Dibakar Acharjee
**Picture researcher:** Sandeep Kumar Guthikonda
**Project coordinator:** Kathy Middleton
**Production coordinator:** Kenneth J. Wright
**Prepress technician:** Kenneth J. Wright
**Print coordinator:** Katherine Berti

**Front Cover:** Statue of Augustus Caesar (left); The Roman Forum (background); Kim Jong-Un; leader of North Korea (top inset); A photograph of Adolf Hitler on October 25, 1936 (bottom inset)
**Title page:** North Korean leader Kim Jong-Un

**Photographs:**
Title page: Ed Jones/AFP/GettyImages; P4: kbuntu/123RF; P5: Diego Goldberg/Sygma/Corbis; P6: Ed Jones/AFP/Getty Images; P7: JIM WATSON/AFP/Getty Images; P8-9: Mart/Shutterstock; P10: Fratelli Alinari/Alinari via Getty Images; P11: Photos.com/Thinkstock; P12: Popperfoto/Getty Images; P13: Keystone-France/Gamma-Keystone via Getty Images; P14: Bettmann/CORBIS; P15: Bettmann/CORBIS; P16: JEWEL SAMAD/AFP/Getty Images; P17: Mohamed Elsayyed / Shutterstock; P18: GOH CHAI HIN/AFP/Getty Images; P19: fotostory / Shutterstock; P20: Sven Creutzmann/Mambo photo/Getty Images; P21: Patrick CASTAGNAS/Gamma-Rapho via Getty Images; P22: Patrick Robert/Corbis; P23: KYODO NEWS/AFP/Getty Images; P24: Vincent Prevost/Hemis/Corbis; P25: ROBERTO SCHMIDT/AFP/Getty Images; P26: velirina/Shutterstock; P27: STRINGER/AFP/Getty Images; P28: ASHRAF SHAZLY/AFP/Getty Images; P29: suronin/Shutterstock; P30: STR/AFP/Getty Images; P31: IVAN SEKRETAREV/AFP/Getty Images; P32: Karl Blackwell/Lonely Planet Images; P33: Tom Stoddart/Getty Images; P34: MARK GRAHAM/AFP/Getty Images; P35: DENIS SINYAKOV/AFP/Getty Images; P36: Jane Sweeney/JAI/Corbis; P37: Hulton Archive/Getty Images; P40: The Egyptian Presidency/Xinhua Press/Corbis; P41: Benjamin Lowy/Edit by Getty Images; P42: Kamira / Shutterstock; P43: Robert Nickelsberg//Time Life Pictures/Getty Images; P44: Hung Chung Chih / Shutterstock; P45: Gerald Bourke/WFP via Getty Image. Thinkstock: front cover (left); Shutterstock: front cover (background); Wikimedia Commons/J Milburn: front cover (inset bottom); David Guttenfelder/AP/dapd: front cover (inset top)

**Library and Archives Canada Cataloguing in Publication**

BBoyle, Sarah B., 1981-
   What is a dictatorship? / Sarah B. Boyle.

(Forms of government)
Includes index.
Issued also in electronic format.
ISBN 978-0-7787-5317-9 (bound).--ISBN 978-0-7787-5324-7 (pbk.)

   1. Dictatorship--Juvenile literature.  I. Title.  II. Series: Forms of government (St. Catharines, Ont.)

JC495.B69 2013          j321.9          C2013-901031-9

**Library of Congress Cataloging-in-Publication Data**

CIP available at Library of Congress

# Crabtree Publishing Company

www.crabtreebooks.com          1-800-387-7650

Printed in the U.S.A./042013/SX20130306

**Published in Canada**
Crabtree Publishing
616 Welland Ave.
St. Catharines, Ontario
L2M 5V6

**Published in the United States**
Crabtree Publishing
PMB 59051
350 Fifth Avenue, 59th Floor
New York, New York 10118

**Published in the United Kingdom**
Crabtree Publishing
Maritime House
Basin Road North, Hove
BN41 1WR

**Published in Australia**
Crabtree Publishing
3 Charles Street
Coburg North
VIC 3058

# CONTENTS

A government is a group of people who work together to rule a country. A government creates and enforces laws. It also provides important services such as running water, medical care, and education. Most countries have a constitution. A constitution is a document that states all the laws that govern a country. It describes who has power and how they can use that power.

## A Powerful Ruler

A dictatorship is a form of government. The leader of a dictatorship is called a dictator. Throughout history, all dictators have been men. In a dictatorship, the dictator has absolute power, or all the power in the country. The dictator does not have to follow laws or respect the wishes of the citizens in the country. Whatever the dictator says becomes the law of the country.

Countries run by dictatorships often do not have a constitution. If the country does have a constitution, the dictator ignores its laws or changes the constitution so he can do what he wants.

Adolf Hitler was the dictator of Germany from 1933 to 1945. He ruled with absolute power.

## Totalitarian Dictatorships

Dictatorships are often **totalitarian** governments. In a totalitarian dictatorship, the dictator controls all aspects of life in the country. These include politics, **economy**, culture, religion, and the private lives of citizens. But not all dictatorships limit freedom. Some dictators are *benevolent*, or nice, rulers. They treat their people well. But even in a benevolent dictatorship, the people's rights are based on the will of the dictator. If he suddenly decides to take these rights away, he has every power to do so.

The military **juntas** of South America were dictatorships run by small groups of military officials. Augusto Pinochet led the junta that ruled Chile in the 1970s.

## The Dictator

Dictatorships are usually run by one powerful leader. Dictators can gain power though family ties. They may **inherit** the position from the previous dictator when he dies. More often, a dictator gets his power by using force or violence. Very often, dictators keep their power by threatening to hurt or kill people who disagree with them. Sometimes they do kill those people.

### Civil Liberties

Civil liberties are the rights guaranteed to a country's citizens by law. These rights include the right to own property, the right to vote, the right to practice a religion, and the right to free speech. Freedom of speech is the right of citizens to say whatever they believe without government punishment. Dictatorships often limit or eliminate many civil liberties.

# A Modern Dictatorship

Kim Il-Sung took over the government of North Korea in 1953. He gradually became a dictator. In the beginning, he had little power. He knew he needed to unite the people of North Korea under him. So he started spreading rumors that the United States government was making North Koreans sick on purpose. Anyone who said that these rumors were untrue was sent to prison camps. Those people were never heard from again. Kim unified the people under him by giving them a common enemy and getting rid of anyone who disagreed with him.

## A Cult of Personality

Kim also encouraged a **cult of personality** to cement his power. He used the **media** to portray himself as all-knowing and the best possible leader in all of North Korea. The people believed he could do no wrong, so no one challenged him. By the late 1950s, Kim had become an absolute dictator. His position as dictator passed from him to his son and eventually to his grandson.

## The Constitution

In North Korea, the dictator is called the supreme leader. The government of North Korea also has a **parliament**, called the Supreme People's Assembly. The supreme leader's political party chooses all candidates for the Supreme People's Assembly. The people vote for the candidates, but often only one candidate is listed on the ballot. Members of this parliament have no real power. The Supreme People's Assembly's only job is to approve the decisions made by the supreme leader. They cannot disagree with him.

Kim Il-Sung is considered North Korea's "eternal president" even though he died in 1994.

Born into a prison camp, Shin Dong-Hyuk was one of the few to escape their horrors. He had eaten little for his entire life and saw his brother shot to death and mother hung. He now speaks around the world to **human rights** organizations.

## Prison Camps and Executions

The government of North Korea uses fear to keep its people under control. It also denies its citizens many freedoms. Anyone who disagrees with the supreme leader is sent to a **re-education camp**. In this camp, they are forced to do **hard labor** until they realize that the supreme leader is always right. If a citizen speaks out against the government over and over, that citizen will get sent to a prison camp for life. North Korea is considered one of the least free countries in the world.

### Cult of Personality

Dictators often create a cult of personality to give themselves more power. They use the newspapers, television stations, and **propaganda** to portray themselves as perfect and godlike.

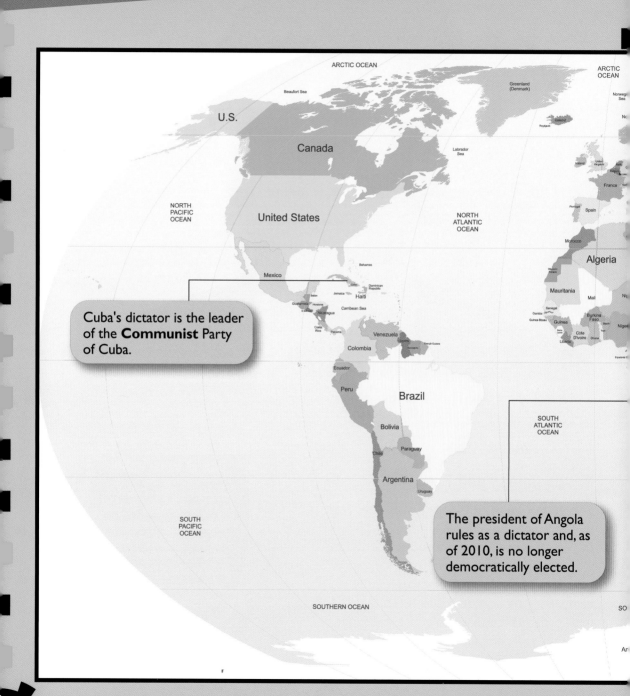

Cuba's dictator is the leader of the **Communist** Party of Cuba.

The president of Angola rules as a dictator and, as of 2010, is no longer democratically elected.

Turkmenistan's dictator is called the president for life. Only one political party is legal.

Uzbekistan remains a **democracy** in name only. The president is continually re-elected because no other candidates are allowed to run against him.

North Korea is a **hereditary** dictatorship, where the supreme leader has absolute power.

Also known as Myanmar, Burma is run by a military dictatorship.

Sudan is an Islamic country with an elected president. He has gradually gained all the political power in the country.

The president of Chad was elected. However, there is no **term limit** on how long he can serve. He has power over most of the government.

# THE FIRST DICTATORS

The first dictators were leaders elected by the citizens of ancient Rome around 500 BCE. They had absolute power, but only for a short period of time. During that period, the Roman senate, or group of lawmakers, gave the dictator a specific job to do. Usually, the dictator had a battle or a war to win. Once he had accomplished his job, he was no longer a dictator and no longer had unlimited power.

## Power Grabber

In 81 BCE, Lucius Cornelius Sulla became the first Roman dictator with no term limit. The senate gave him unlimited power so he could oversee the writing of new laws and a new constitution. During this time, Sulla used his power to get rid of anyone who disagreed with him and to get rich. After a year as dictator, he resigned from the position. By 44 BCE, the Roman senate eliminated the position of dictator. The position was just too powerful.

## From Emperor to Dictator

Napoleon Bonaparte was emperor of France from 1804 to 1815. He began his political career as a general in the French army. He then used the army to stage a **coup d'état**. Napoleon named himself first consul, the head of the French government. He got rid of people who disagreed with him and slowly gained more power. In 1804, Napoleon crowned himself emperor of France.

Lucius Cornelius Sulla killed people who disagreed with how he ran the Roman government. Then he took those people's property and money for himself and his loyal followers.

| 500 BCE | First dictator ruled in ancient Rome |
|---|---|
| 81 BCE | Lucius Cornelius Sulla became "Dictator for Life" in ancient Rome |
| 49 BCE | Julius Caesar last dictator in ancient Rome |
| 1804–1815 | Napoleon Bonaparte emperor of France |

Napoleon was the most powerful man on the European continent in the early 1800s. He led the French army to many military victories.

Napoleon used his military experience and position as emperor to expand France's power in Europe. He fought a number of wars now called the Napoleonic Wars. In these wars, France conquered most of Europe. Napoleon ruled with absolute power until he lost the Battle of Waterloo to the British and their allies in 1815. The **monarchy** was then restored in France. Napoleon spent the rest of his life living on a small island. He was never allowed to return to France.

## Coup d'État

A coup d'état is sometimes simply called a coup. In a coup, a dictator leads a small group of people who are part of the existing government. They then overthrow the government by using violence. After the coup, the dictator is the new leader of the government.

# THE AGE OF DICTATORS

The 1900s are sometimes called the age of dictators. During that time, many dictators ruled throughout the world. Adolf Hitler is perhaps history's most famous dictator. He took over Germany in 1933. He led the world into **World War II** and killed more than 11 million people. When Hitler lost World War II in 1945, he also lost his power.

## Lethal Leaders

Other dictators of the 1900s include Benito Mussolini. He was dictator of Italy from 1930 to 1943. He used his **secret police** to kill people who disagreed with him. Joseph Stalin was dictator of the **Soviet Union** from 1941 to 1953. Stalin used prison camps called *gulags*, **executions**, and mass shootings to get rid of political **opposition**. He killed as many as 20 million people during his time in power.

Even if a prisoner avoided execution in a Soviet Union gulag, he was likely to die from hard labor.

### Stalin's *Gulag*

The term *gulag* originally referred to the Soviet Union's system of prison camps. Today the term is used to describe any prison that houses political prisoners and forces them to do hard labor. North Korea's prison camps are sometimes known as the North Korean gulags.

# Dictators in Asia

Mao Zedong was the leader of China from 1949 until his death in 1976. A totalitarian dictator, he had a plan to make China a world power. He called it the Great Leap Forward. It created large, state-controlled farms. Unfortunately, these farms did not produce enough food to feed all the Chinese. Mao was successful in making China an international power. But millions of Chinese citizens starved to death because of his policies.

The dictator Pol Pot ruled Cambodia from 1975 to 1979. He forced the people to work on **collective farms** and on forced labor projects. Like other dictators, he executed those who disagreed with him. During his three-year rule, more than 20 percent of the citizens of Cambodia died.

After the Great Leap Forward, Mao began the Cultural Revolution in 1966. He urged university and high school students to drop out of school and join a military group called the Red Guard. They attacked middle-class people and scholars.

# Modern-Day Dictators

Present-day dictators are mostly in Asia and Africa. These dictatorships often call themselves democracies, and their leader calls himself a president. Some go so far as to allow their citizens to participate in elections. But the rulers of these countries behave like dictators and do not allow their citizens many freedoms.

| 1930–1943 | Benito Mussolini was dictator of Italy |
|---|---|
| 1933–1945 | Adolf Hitler was dictator of Germany |
| 1939–1975 | Francisco Franco was dictator of Spain |
| 1941–1953 | Joseph Stalin was dictator of the Soviet Union |
| 1949–1976 | Mao Zedong was dictator of China |
| 1975–1979 | Pol Pot was dictator in Cambodia |
| 1948–present | North Korea ruled by hereditary dictatorship |

# VARIETIES OF DICTATORSHIPS

Dictatorships can be organized in many different ways. Some dictators have clear and absolute power. Other dictators rule countries that call themselves democracies. However, the elections are set up so that only the dictator can win. Governments such as these are really dictatorships.

## The Benevolent Dictator

Sometimes, but not often, a dictator uses his power to help the people of his country instead of himself. These rulers are called benevolent dictators. Giuseppe Garibaldi was a benevolent dictator. He took control of Italy in 1860 to unite its various **city-states**. He used his position to guarantee a better life for the people. Once Italy was united, he gave up his power.

## Single-Party Dictatorships

Other dictatorships are single-party states. A political party is a group of people who share the same ideas about how to govern a country. In a single-party state, there is only one political party. All other political parties are illegal. The head of that sole political party becomes the leader of the entire country. For example, China was a single-party state by the early 1950s. The Communist Party of China was the only legal political party. Mao was the chairman of the Communist Party. Because he was the chairman, he was the leader of the entire Chinese government.

Giuseppe Garibaldi declared himself "Dictator of Sicily" in 1860 to unite Italy. He is considered an Italian hero.

When the military junta took over Chile, its leaders were supposed to take turns being head of the country. But Pinochet made his job as leader permanent.

## Military Dictatorship

A military dictatorship is lead by the leader of the country's military. Often this leader uses the military to stage a coup d'état. Some dictators in South America in the 1900s were leaders of military juntas. In a military junta, a small group of military officers acts as dictator. Chile was run by a military junta from 1973 to 1990.

When the junta took over the government of Chile, General Augusto Pinochet was the leader. He ruled Chile as army general and dictator from 1973 until 1990. Pinochet used the military to threaten people who spoke out against him. By controlling the military, he was able to hold onto his power for almost two decades.

### After Dictatorship

In 2004, the Chilean government placed Augusto Pinochet under house arrest. He was confined to his home instead of being held in a prison. When he died in 2006, he was being charged in over 300 criminal court cases. The government accused him of killing political opponents and stealing money from the government.

# CHANGING DICTATORSHIPS

A government in transition changes from one form of government to another. Burma is a good example of a dictatorship in transition. The military had been in control since a coup d'état in 1962.

## From Dictatorship to Democracy

The Burmese have protested for democracy throughout the dictatorship's rule. The National League for Democracy led many of these protests. Aung San Suu Kyi took a leading role in this organization. In 1990, the National League won over 80 percent of the seats in the Burmese Parliament. However, the military dictatorship never allowed those elected leaders to take their positions. The military dictatorship used violence to stop the protests. Many protesters were killed over the 40 years of military rule. However, as of 2010, the government began many political **reforms**. It is working toward democracy and free elections.

The government of Burma has not explained why it is allowing more democracy. The government's critics suspect it is just making it look as though it wants to create a democracy in the country. They think the government will keep ruling the same way it always has. But the citizens continue to fight for a democratic government. Burma is slowly moving from dictatorship to democracy.

In 1991, Aung San Suu Kyi won the Nobel Peace Prize, an award given to honor people's work in promoting peace. The Burmese government would not allow her to personally accept her prize until 2012.

### Aung San Suu Kyi

Aung San Suu Kyi has long fought for democracy in Burma. The military junta placed Suu Kyi under house arrest for more than 15 years for speaking out for democracy. She was finally released in 2010 after years of protest and international pressure. Suu Kyi now serves in Burma's parliament.

## Congo: The Struggle for Democracy

The government of the Democratic Republic of the Congo is also in transition. Mobutu Sese Seko was a dictator in the country from 1965 to 1997. In 1997, a **rebellion** successfully removed Mobutu from power. A period of civil war followed. In 2005, the country passed a new constitution. This constitution promised a **separation of powers** among the three branches of government. Congo is in the process of creating democratic policies after decades of dictatorship.

Egyptian protesters brought down their president in 2011. The dictator Hosni Mubarak had controlled all branches of government and severely restricted the media.

## Egypt: A Temporary Dictatorship?

Sometimes when a country is in transition from one form of government to another, a dictator takes charge to bring order to the country quickly. In 2011, the people of Egypt staged protests for democracy. They succeeded in getting the dictator, President Hosni Mubarak, to step down.

In 2012, Egyptians elected Mohammed Morsi as president. But he has since taken all the power in the government and rules like a dictator. He claims he is keeping that power to make sure people are safe while the government is changing. Once the political situation calms down, he says he will stop being a dictator.

# RIGHTS OF THE PEOPLE

Often dictators attempt to control all aspects of their citizens' lives. As a result, people in a dictatorship often have very few rights. The rights they do have are given at the **whim** of the dictator. Whenever he wishes to take those rights away, he can.

## North Korea and Human Rights

The people of North Korea have very few rights. They do not have freedom of speech. The government owns all the news organizations. It controls what is reported so the country does not have a free press.

North Korea is officially an **atheist** state. People do not have freedom of religion and cannot freely practice their chosen religion. The government uses threats of arrest and violence to stop people from practicing any religion.

Even worse, the citizens have no protection from government violence. People who disagree with the government are taken to prison camps. They work like slaves in these camps. They may also be tortured or executed. International organizations such as Amnesty International and Human Rights Watch condemn North Korea as having one of the worst human rights records in the world.

North Koreans regularly do not have enough food to eat. Many starve.

President Gurbanguly Berdimuhamedov won 97 percent of the vote in the 2012 elections in Turkmenistan. No other candidates were allowed to run.

## Democracy in Name Only

Some dictatorships appear to grant many rights to their citizens. These dictatorships look like democracies. The constitution promises many freedoms, such as freedom of speech and of the press. The country holds elections, and the people vote for the leader.

Though the constitution guarantees civil liberties, the government does not actually allow them. It uses violence and the threat of prison to silence opposition. The country has elections, but they are not free and fair.

For example, Turkmenistan's constitution promises that the people may form political parties. But the government does not allow any opposition candidates to run in the elections. The president wins every election because he is the only candidate.

### Protecting People

Amnesty International and Human Rights Watch are two organizations that work to protect human rights around the world. They write reports and **lobby** governments to make changes when people are being abused. The organizations watch dictatorships, such as those in North Korea, closely. Their goal is to make sure all people have the same basic human rights, no matter what country they live in.

Citizens in a dictatorship have to follow the orders and laws of the dictator. Dictators use their citizens as one more tool to get what they want: power and wealth. Citizens are expected to do as they are told and to support the dictator, no matter what.

## Socialism and Dictatorship

Socialism is a way of organizing an economy. In a socialist country, the government owns most of the agriculture and industry. The government then employs citizens. It is the citizens' role to do the job the government assigns to them. They do not choose their own career. This system allows the government to keep the country's farms and factories running smoothly. They often produce enough food and goods to support the country's population. The government distributes the goods and food equally among all citizens. But the people do not have the freedom to pursue their own dreams and desires.

Some dictatorships are socialist countries. But in a dictatorship, the dictator will not distribute the profits equally. He will keep more for himself and his loyal supporters. In socialist dictatorships, the people often do not have enough food to survive. But they still must work at the jobs assigned to them by the dictator. They cannot work at a different job to make more money.

President Raul Castro is the dictator of Cuba. He inherited his position from his brother Fidel Castro, who ruled Cuba for almost 50 years.

### Cuban Cigars

Cuba is a socialist dictatorship. The country is famous for its cigars. The government owns all the cigar factories and employs the workers in those factories. The Cuban cigar business makes a lot of money. Even though the country is socialist, most of the citizens do not get a share of this wealth. They continue to live in poverty.

Burma's military upholds the dictatorship's power.

## The Military

One of the most important roles a citizen can play in a dictatorship is as a soldier in the military. In a military dictatorship, the government uses the military to keep the citizens under control.

Typically dictatorships require all male citizens to serve two or more years in the military. Cuba demands that men and women aged 17 and older serve two years. In North Korea, men may have to spend up to ten years in the military.

Members of the military often have more rights and luxuries than other citizens. They may have more money, better food, and nicer cars or homes.

In exchange, the soldiers have to carry out the will of the dictator. This can mean killing other citizens, arresting political protesters, and guarding prisoners. These soldiers pay a high price for their luxuries.

# A DICTATOR IS MADE

**D**ictators usually gain power by taking it. They may take control of a country all at once or they may do so gradually. A dictator may stage a coup d'état, influence elections illegally, or inherit his power.

Idriss Déby is president of Chad. But he acts more like a dictator than a president.

## Elections and Dictatorships

Some dictators come to power by using elections. But these elections are not free or fair. For example, the citizens in Chad elect a president and members of the legislative assembly every five years. But the same man, President Idriss Déby, has won every election since 1996. Many people in Chad believe Déby uses his power to rig elections. When someone rigs an election, they guarantee a certain person will win. It does not matter whether the people actually voted for that person or not.

## Slowly Gaining Power

Dictators can also take their power gradually. They begin in a position with limited power. Then they gather more and more control in the country. For example, in 1933, the president of Germany appointed Adolf Hitler as **chancellor**. Over the next year, Hitler and his Nazi party got rid of local governments. They passed laws that gave all the power in the country to Hitler. By 1934, Hitler was the dictator of Germany.

### Saudi Arabia

Saudi Arabia has a hereditary dictatorship. All the leaders of Saudi Arabia since the 1930s have been members of the same royal family, called the House of Saud. Everyone in it is related to the first king of Saudi Arabia, Ibn Saud.

Kim Jong-Il had an elaborate funeral. Tens of thousands of North Koreans showed up to mourn his death.

## Hereditary Dictatorship

Some countries have a hereditary dictatorship. When something is hereditary, it is passed down from a parent to a child. In a hereditary dictatorship, the dictator passes his power down to his son. For example, North Korea's Supreme Leader Kim Il-Sung passed his power down to his son, Kim Jong-Il. Then Kim Jong-Il named his son, Kim Jong-Un, to be the next leader.

## Leader of the Party

In a single-party state, the ruling political party chooses a leader. That leader becomes the leader of the country. In China, the only party is the Communist Party of China. The party meets every five years to decide on major political issues. They choose the leader of their party. Whoever leads the Communist Party leads the entire country of China.

# In Charge

The most important political figure in a dictatorship is the dictator himself. He may rule with the power of his personality, with his people following him willingly. Or he may create laws that force the people to support his rule, whether they want to or not.

## Charismatic Dictator

Some dictators rule based on the power of their own personality. Hitler was extremely **charismatic**. When he spoke, the German people were drawn to him.

The people of Germany believed everything Hitler said. He was able to use his charisma and the force of his speeches to unite the people behind him. They followed him into war.

Other dictators are not as charismatic. These dictators create a cult of personality. Kim Il-Sung of North Korea went to great lengths to make his people see him as a hero. He had beautiful portraits of himself hung in every train station in North Korea. Both Hitler and Kim Il-Sung were powerful dictators because their people believed they were heroes.

Supreme Leader Kim Il-Sung had more than 500 statues of himself erected around the country.

In 2010, election monitors made sure the voting in Sudan was fair and free.

## A False Position

The dictators of the 2000s often call themselves presidents. These leaders rule countries that have constitutions. But these leaders write or rewrite their countries' constitutions to give themselves more power. In countries such as Sudan, the president writes laws or rewrites the constitution. He gains more power for himself this way. Sudanese President Omar al-Bashir created a new government office that writes laws. These laws guarantee that he and his party would win any elections.

The president of Angola also acts like a dictator. President José Eduardo dos Santos was elected in 1979. In 2010, he and his party rewrote Angola's constitution. That constitution ended presidential elections. Dos Santos rewrote the constitution to give himself the powers of a dictator.

### Election Monitoring

Many people in the international community are trying to stop men, such as Omar al-Bashir, from unfairly winning elections. When they suspect a leader is going to try to rig an election, they go to that country to monitor the election. They watch the casting and counting of votes. They hope this careful watching will make rigging the election impossible.

Governments are complex organizations. Many people must work together to govern a country. To make governing easier, governments are often divided into three branches: the executive, legislative, and judicial branches.

## The Executive Branch

The executive branch is run by the leader of the entire country. In a dictatorship, the executive branch is the most powerful branch of government. It is headed by the dictator. The executive branch is responsible for making sure all citizens obey the country's laws. In a dictatorship, the executive branch also often writes those laws or controls lawmakers who do. The executive branch may also control the country's court system. Dictators may appoint judges or have the power to approve or **veto** the judges' decisions.

The palace for the president of Turkmenistan cost more than $250 million dollars. Its price shows the power of the executive branch. Most people in Turkmenistan live in poverty.

Defendants wait for their trial in the Supreme Court of Uzbekistan. Uzbekistan's president for life has complete control over the country's judiciary.

## The Legislative Branch

The legislative branch is responsible for making laws. Usually, the legislative branch is a group of lawmakers. Many dictatorships today have parliaments that meet regularly to write and vote on laws. The members of these parliaments may be elected or the dictator may appoint them. Either way, they usually do not have the final word on the laws of the country. The dictator has the power to approve or veto any law they write. And if the dictator does not think the lawmakers are doing a good job, he can remove them from their position. Though some dictatorships have legislative bodies, they rarely have any real power over the country.

## The Judicial Branch

The final branch of government is the judicial branch. This branch includes all the courts and judges in the country. This branch's job is to interpret laws. It makes judgments when it sees that those laws have been broken. In a dictatorship, the **judiciary** is often a part of the executive branch. The dictator appoints judges. Those judges are expected to carry out the dictator's wishes. The dictator uses the judiciary to enforce laws and send political opponents to jail.

# LOCAL GOVERNMENTS

Governments are often divided into three levels. These levels include federal, regional, and local governments. The federal government is the national government. Its laws apply to the entire country. The country is then split into different regions. Regional governments are responsible for governing these areas. Finally, each region is divided again into smaller areas that are governed by the local government. The regional and local governments are smaller than the federal government.

They are responsible for taking care of local problems. In dictatorships, regional and local governments must obey the laws of the federal government. These laws are created by the dictator.

Members of local and regional governments remain subject to the whims of the dictator. Dictators use local and regional governments to extend their power throughout their countries.

In 2011, Sudan split into two countries—Sudan and South Sudan. Councils of ministers must deal with some issues left from that division.

## The Federal Government

The federal government is responsible for the entire country. Only the federal government can meet with foreign countries or declare war. And only the federal government can create and rule the armed forces. A dictator is in charge of the federal government in a dictatorship.

City leaders meet in the city hall of Yangon, which was once the capital of Burma.

## Sudan's Regional Governments

The regional government of Sudan is under the direct control of the president. Sudan has 26 states. Each of those states has its own regional government with a governor and a council of ministers. The members of the regional government in Sudan are either appointed or elected. The president appoints the legislative branch, called the council of ministers. He also chooses three candidates for governor. The people of the region then elect their governor from those choices.

## The *Hluttaws* of Burma

Burma has a complex system of local and regional governments. There are seven state governments, seven regional governments, and six divisions and zones. A specific ethnic group lives in each of these six geographic areas. Members of that ethnic group are guaranteed the right to participate in its government. Each of these state, regional, and local governments has its own *hluttaw*.

The *hluttaw* is a legislative body. Citizens elect three-fourths of the members of this body. But most of these elected representatives are members of the Union Solidarity and Development Party. The government must approve of these members. So party members are likely to govern how the military junta wants them to govern. The other fourth of the *hluttaw* are members of the military chosen directly by the military junta. The junta controls, either directly or indirectly, the members of the local *hluttaws*.

In a dictatorship, laws are made one of two ways. The dictator himself may issue laws by decree. A decree is an official order from a ruler or other authority. Sometimes, as in North Korea, the legislative body supposedly has the power to approve or veto the laws issued by the dictator. But in reality, they never veto a law. Their only option is to approve the law. In other dictatorships, the legislative body writes laws. In this situation, the dictator has the power to approve or veto the law. However laws are made in a dictatorship, the dictator's opinion about a law is the final word.

## A Dictator of Many Roles

In Turkmenistan, the dictator serves as president. He is also the supreme leader of the National Assembly—the highest legislative body in the country. These positions make him head of the executive and the legislative branches. The president must also approve every candidate for the National Assembly before he or she is allowed to run for the office. Thus the president has almost complete control over every law that is passed in the country.

The Supreme People's Assembly of North Korea is the country's legislative body.

# The Courts: One More Tool

Courts interpret the laws and determine if a law has been broken. The courts in a dictatorship are usually under the direct power of the dictator.

In North Korea, the constitution states that the courts are independent. This means that no one, not even the supreme leader, can influence them. But, in reality, the supreme leader has complete control over the courts. He has often already told the judge how to rule before a trial even begins. The courts send people to jail, where they are often tortured. Sometimes they sentence people to public execution. By controlling the courts, the supreme leader is able to control everyone who disagrees with him.

President Islam Karimov of Uzbekistan has almost complete control over the country's judicial branch. An international organization, the United Nations found torture commonly used in the judiciary.

## Trial at Court

When someone is brought to trial, they appear before a judge in court. The judge hears what happened, then decides whether the person has broken the law. In dictatorships, trials are often unfair. The judge has made a decision before the trial begins. The dictator uses the courts to show what happens when citizens disobey him: jail, torture, or death.

The country of Uzbekistan has a **corrupt** court system. The constitution gives the president the power to appoint all of the country's judges. The president appoints people who agree with him and will carry out his will. This power gives the resident complete control over the courts. Another problem with the courts in Uzbekistan is that the **prosecutors** also investigate the crimes. They only collect evidence that will help them convict suspects. Any evidence that would have proven their innocence is left out of the trial. It is almost impossible for people to get fair trials.

Some dictatorships base their country's economy on socialism while others allow **capitalism**. In a capitalist economy, citizens own and run their own businesses. Dictatorships often limit capitalism because it allows citizens to make a lot of money and grow more powerful. Often dictators use their power to grab their country's wealth for themselves.

## Cuba's State-Controlled Economy

Cuba is a socialist country. The government owns and controls most of the industry and agriculture. The government also employs most Cuban citizens. It sets the prices of goods, then rations those goods. When a government rations goods, it limits how much an individual person is allowed to buy. When this system works, all the citizens in the country have what they need to survive. Unfortunately, Cuba has had problems with getting enough food for all its citizens. Cuba's dictatorship has slowly allowed more capitalist businesses to develop. They help close the gap between what the government can provide and what the people need.

Cuba is allowing some farmers to grow crops on their own time and land. The farmers sell these crops in a few, small, local markets.

Farmers cultivate cotton in Chad. They may make more money from their crops in the future.

## Uzbekistan: The Dictator Keeps It All

Uzbekistan is rich in natural resources. It has the fourth-largest gold deposits in the world. It also has lots of natural gas and oil. The government owns these resources and the mining companies that produce them. Unlike Cuba, the government of Uzbekistan does not try to provide its people with all they need. The government gives all the profits from selling its natural resources to a small group of people. This situation makes the people who rule the country very rich and the citizens very poor.

## Chad: A Struggling People

The government of Chad controls its major industries, including oil production and the cotton industry. Though these make money, most of the citizens of Chad are poor. The government is in the process of giving up ownership of the cotton industry. Soon the citizens will own it for themselves. This change will allow citizens to more directly benefit from their own work. They will collect the profits of the industry directly, instead of waiting for the government to distribute the profits.

# THE POWER OF THE MEDIA

**M**edia refers to organizations that spread news among people. Media organizations can be very powerful. The information they report gives citizens the ability to understand their government and form opinions about it. Dictators often control the media. They do not allow it to report stories that would make their citizens turn against the government. They often use the media to paint their governments as good and helpful to the citizens, even if they are not.

## State-Controlled Media

The North Korean government tightly controls the country's media. The constitution gives people freedom of speech. It also promises freedom of the press. But the government does not respect these rights. It keeps the media from reporting stories it dislikes. It is only allowed to report stories that make the government look good. The supreme leader of North Korea often uses the media to spread spectacular stories about himself. These stories contribute to his image in North Korea as an almost godlike figure.

The supreme leaders of North Korea cannot control the media outside of their country. The foreign media's view of these leaders is quite different than North Korea's.

Uzbekistan's dictatorship sent in the military to shut down the 2005 protests. It also did not allow the media to cover the story.

## Uzbekistan: Silencing the Opposition

The government of Uzbekistan owns and controls all the major media organizations. These organizations must report stories that show the president and his government favorably, or they do not report on politics at all. The government does not allow any opposition parties to use the media. Opposition parties who distribute their own media may be jailed or sentenced to death. The government's control of the media means the citizens do not hear any opinions that are different from those of the president.

In 2005, citizens in Andijan, Uzbekistan, protested against the government. The military shot and killed more than 150 citizens to stop the protests. But the government did not allow the media to cover the story. By stopping media coverage, the government was able to stop the protests from spreading. The government's tight control over the media allows the president to maintain power over the country.

### Radio Jamming in North Korea

Radio waves cross international borders easily. North Korean citizens could easily hear news from South Korea or China. But the North Korean government does not want its citizens to hear any news from other countries. So it *jams* radio signals. This process cancels out any radio waves that come from a station not approved by the North Korean government.

Food, clothing, music, art, religion, language, rules for behavior, values, and beliefs: these things make up a country's culture. To most people, culture seems to be something that is always there. It gets passed down through families for many years. But dictators often try to create a culture that will help them keep their power. Instead of relying on the traditions of their country, they create new customs. These new traditions unite the people behind them. Dictators use culture as one more tool to control their people.

Turkmenistan President for Life Saparmurat Niyazov had statues of himself erected all around the country.

## Creating a Cult of Personality

In Turkmenistan, President for Life Saparmurat Niyazov used the education system to help spread his cult of personality. He required all schoolchildren to read his book as their main course of study. He had portraits of himself placed all over the country. Wherever a citizen goes in Turkmenistan, he is reminded of how powerful and amazing the dictator is.

## China: The Cultural Revolution

Some dictators go even farther than creating a culture that supports their rule. They outlaw traditional culture. This move forces citizens to embrace the new culture of the dictatorship. While Mao was a dictator in China, he started the Cultural Revolution. This movement made it nearly impossible for Chinese people to practice their traditional religions. The government closed down churches and temples and encouraged the citizens to become atheists.

Mao's "Little Red Book" was read by thousands and thousands of Chinese citizens during the Cultural Revolution.

In place of the old traditions, the dictator Mao Zedong created Maoism. This set of beliefs told the people that they should work together to overthrow capitalism. If they worked together, everybody would have equality and live in peace. Mao used these beliefs to keep his people united and working hard. Many Chinese citizens during that time were poor farmers. But if they continued to work hard and follow the rules, Maoism told them their lives would get better. Maoism was a way of life for the Chinese until Mao's death in 1976.

### Mao's "Little Red Book"

In 1965, the government of China published a book with a bright red cover called *Quotations from Chairman Mao Zedong*. It contained quotations from Mao's writings and public speeches about Maoism. Citizens all over China carried it around with them. They read it at every spare moment. It was very important in spreading the culture of Maoism.

# Forms of Government

| | Democracy | Dictatorship |
|---|---|---|
| **Basis of power** | People elect officials to represent their views and beliefs. | The dictator controls everything in the country. His word is the law. |
| **Rights of people** | People have many rights, including the right to fair and free elections, the right to assemble, and the right to choose how to live their lives. | The people have very few rights. Their duty is to do whatever the dictator wants. |
| **How leaders are chosen** | Frequent and regular elections are held to vote for leaders. | Leaders can inherit their position or take it with military force. The most powerful political party may also choose them. |
| **Basis of judicial branch** | A separate judicial branch enforces the laws made by the legislative branch. Laws are supposed to be enforced freely and fairly. | The judicial branch does what the dictator wants. |
| **Relation of business to the form of government** | Government plays a limited role in businesses. They may charge taxes and make some laws to make sure businesses are run fairly. | The government often owns the major businesses in a country. |
| **Control of media** | The government does not control the media. People have access to many opinions and diverse information from the media. | The dictator either tells the media what to report or **censors** the media's reports. |
| **Role of religion** | People may choose to practice their own religion. | People may or may not be able to practice their religion freely. However, political parties and focus on the dictator's personality are more important than religion. |

| Monarchy | Oligarchy | Theocracy |
|---|---|---|
| A monarch's power is inherited from a previous generation. In **absolute monarchies**, monarchs are believed to be chosen by God. | A select few use their wealth or secret connections to powerful people in the government to control the country. They are rarely elected. | The government is based on the state religion. |
| Rights are not guaranteed in an absolute monarchy. In a **constitutional monarchy**, rights are outlined in the country's constitution. | No rights are guaranteed, but in elected **oligarchies**, citizens can vote. | The laws of the state religion limit the rights of the people. |
| Power is passed down through families. Monarchies have different rules for who inherits power. In constitutional monarchies, the leaders of governing bodies, such as a parliament, are chosen through elections. | Oligarchs take power in most cases. They are rarely elected. They usually lead hidden behind the government. | Leaders are elected or appointed or chosen by religious customs. |
| In absolute monarchies, monarchs run the courts. Most constitutional monarchies have a separate judicial branch to ensure fair treatment. | Most oligarchies hide behind regular government functions. With their money and power, they affect the judicial branch's decisions. | All laws are based on the state religion. The judicial branch bases its judgments on that religion's laws. |
| Leaders of absolute monarchies control all of the wealth of a country. In constitutional monarchies, decisions about business are made by a governing body, such as a parliament. | Many oligarchs control wealthy businesses. | Businesses can be owned by citizens or by the government. |
| The press is not free in an absolute monarchy. Many constitutional monarchies, however, guarantee freedom of the media and speech. | Oligarchs tend to own and control all the media. | The media can be controlled by the government or by private citizens. It must follow the laws of the state religion. |
| Absolute monarchies often require people to have the same religion as the monarch. Many constitutional monarchies guarantee freedom of religion. | Some oligarchs share a common religion. | Religion forms the basis of the government. It dictates most aspects of the citizens' lives. |

# ASSESSING DICTATORSHIPS

## Here are some of the advantages of a dictatorship.

- Dictators keep the citizens of a country under control. There is often very little political opposition or disorder in a dictatorship. The citizens follow the rules and laws of the dictator. The country is safe as a result.

- Dictatorships can be very stable forms of government. The same ruler leads the country for long periods of time. The citizens know what to expect and how to behave.

- If protests arise and the government seems to be losing control, dictators can stop them very quickly. Because they have absolute power, dictators can halt any violence and impose order. They do not have to wait for the other branches of government to act. They simply do what is necessary as soon as possible.

### President Mohamed Morsi

In 2012, Egyptian President Mohamed Morsi began acting as a dictator. He said it was to ensure the safety of the Egyptian people. But his power grab has resulted in sometimes-violent protests in Egypt.

Egyptian president Mohamed Morsi took over the government of Egypt. He wanted to stop the violent protests and political unrest in the country.

Dictator Muammar Gaddafi ruled Libya until 2011. In 2011, the opposition used violence to force Gaddafi to step down. Thousands were killed in the violence.

## Dictatorship's Disadvantages

Dictatorship has many disadvantages, too.

- Citizens in a dictatorship have very few rights. Often the dictator controls all aspects of the citizens' lives. Dictators often limit freedom of speech, freedom of the press, freedom of religion, and other common civil liberties.

- Citizens have no way to participate meaningfully in their governments. Their votes and voices mean little. The dictator has all the power. He does not share it with anyone.

- There is very little disagreement in a dictatorship. Citizens cannot disagree with their government or do anything to change it. And often they are not allowed to leave the country either.

If they choose to publicly disagree with a dictator, they risk being jailed or killed. Their families may be threatened as well.

- Dictators often control the major industries in a country. They make most of the money in the economy. Citizens are often very poor and cannot participate fully in the economy.

- Though dictatorships can be stable, they can also be violent and unstable. If a dictator came to power by using force or violence, he will often fall from power when someone else challenges him violently. Failed coups can lead to civil war, which is devastating for the people of the country.

# DICTATORS AND THEIR PEOPLE

Dictators have absolute power over their countries. In the past, leaders proudly called themselves dictators. Hitler and other dictators of the 1900s, as well as their citizens, thought that dictatorship was the government of the future. But these men abused their power, and their citizens suffered.

Today, dictators hide behind names such as "president" and "supreme leader" because they do not want people to think of them as totalitarian dictators. But they behave the same way dictators in the 1900s did. They take power and keep it for themselves, at the cost of their citizens' freedom.

## Challenges Facing Dictatorships

Very few dictators take care of their citizens. Usually, their people are poor and often hungry. Dictatorships also limit their citizens' rights. They give citizens only one way to live. Citizens in dictatorships often live in fear that they will offend the dictator and be punished. They have no say in how their country is run.

Many countries around the world do not approve of the way dictators run their countries. They believe people deserve civil liberties and have a right to pursue the lives they want. They pressure dictators by refusing to trade with them. Without these trade goods, such as food and oil, dictators find it even harder to take care of their citizens.

Despite its poverty, downtown Havana, Cuba, is known for its colorful cars and its cultural attractions.

Profits from lead mining in Uzbekistan flow directly to a small group of people. At least one-fourth of the country's people live in poverty.

If trade sanctions fail, sometimes other countries use their military forces to overthrow a dictator. They then put a democratic government in his place.

Many citizens living under dictatorships also want democratic governments. With growing access to the Internet, more and more people can learn about their country and the nations outside their borders. They can see that their leader does not respect their rights and that other countries' leaders do. These people protest against their dictator, demanding that he step down. Sometimes these protests lead to violence or civil war. The challenge for dictatorships moving into the future will be maintaining control over citizens despite growing demands for freedom.

## Rights under Pinochet

When Pinochet was dictator of Chile, he got rid of the constitution and the congress. He also censored the press. He outlawed political activity. The people of Chile were not allowed to form political parties. They could not say anything critical about the government or participate in the government at all.

# DICTATORSHIPS' DOCUMENTS

**P**eople all over China read these *"Quotations from Chairman Mao Zedong"*, as well as others, in Mao's "Little Red Book." The book has also influenced socialists around the world.

"Who are our enemies? Who are our friends? This is a question of the first importance for the **revolution**. The basic reason why all previous revolutionary struggles in China achieved so little was their failure to unite with real friends in order to attack real enemies. A revolutionary party is the guide of the masses, and no revolution ever succeeds when the revolutionary party leads them astray. To ensure that we will definitely achieve success in our revolution and will not lead the masses astray, we must pay attention to uniting with our real friends in order to attack our real enemies...

"In times of difficulty we must not lose sight of our achievements, must see the bright future and must pluck up our courage...

"What is work? Work is struggle. There are difficulties and problems in those places for us to overcome and solve. We go there to work and struggle to overcome these difficulties. A good comrade is one who is more eager to go where the difficulties are greater."

For many Chinese people, Mao Zedong is still a symbol of power and strength. For others, he is a symbol of mass death from starvation and cultural revolution.

Because of starvation, many North Korean children are underweight and short for their age. The World Food Programme sends supplies to North Korean children and mothers to help make up for the lack of food in the country.

## A Matter of Survival

The following paragraphs are from a report by Human Rights Watch about the risk of starvation in North Korea. The dictatorship in North Korea has failed to feed its citizens before, and Human Rights Watch is afraid wide-scale **famine** will happen again.

### I. Summary

"In the mid to late 1990s North Koreans experienced a famine that killed an estimated one million people, or about 5 percent of the population. Hundreds of thousands of others fled to China to find food for themselves and their families. Many who survived suffered long-lasting or permanent damage to their health. Although conditions in North Korea have improved since that time, the North Korean government seems today to be reverting to many of the policies that contributed to the famine...

"North Korea has long used rationing as a means to control its population. By banning people from buying and selling grain, it has forced them to rely on the state for their most basic needs... Under this system, North Koreans could generally only receive state ration coupons through their places of work or study... The government has a long history of distributing food first to trusted citizens, stocking some as part of its "war-preparation storage," and only then distributing the rest through the PDS [Public Distribution System], even if some or many North Koreans go hungry in the process."

# GLOSSARY

**absolute monarchies** Governments in which rulers control every aspect of government. Rule is passed along family lines.

**atheist** A person who does not believe in God

**capitalism** An economic system in which land, factories, and other ways of producing goods are owned and controlled by individuals instead of the government

**censors** Prevents publication or deletes ideas that cause offense or go against the government's views and goals

**chancellor** A high official or head of government

**charismatic** Having a personal appeal that inspires a special loyalty in others

**city-states** Areas, made up of a city and the surrounding region, that govern themselves

**collective farms** A group of several farms owned and operated by the government

**Communist** Someone who believes in system of government in which a single party controls all businesses and agriculture. Under communism, all property is supposed to be publicly owned, and people work and are paid according to their abilities.

**constitutional monarchy** A system of government in which a king, queen, or sultan shares power usually with an elected government

**corrupt** Willing to be dishonest in exchange for money or personal gain

**coup d'état** A sudden overthrow of the government

**cult of personality** A plan to improve the people's view of the personality of a leader, through media and other means, so that a community thinks of the leader as a national hero.

**democracy** A government that is run by the people who live under it. Citizens elect leaders who represent their views.

**economy** The way a nation manages its money, land, workers, and natural resources to produce, buy, and sell goods and services

**executions** The killing of people who have been judged to be guilty of a crime

**famine** An extreme lack a food throughout an area or country

**hard labor** Heavy work with one's hands as a punishment

**hereditary** Passed on from one generation to the next

**human rights** Freedoms that all people should be allowed to have

**inherit** To get from one's parent

**judiciary** A system of courts of laws and their judges

**juntas** Groups of people controlling governments, especially after a revolution

**lobby** To work to persuade members of a legislative group to vote a certain way

**media** Systems of communication designed to reach a large number of people. Media organizations, such as newspapers, magazines, television, and the Internet, report news.

**monarchy** A government by a king, queen, sultan, or other monarch. Rule is passed along family lines.

**oligarchies** Governments in which a small group exercises control. Wealth and power is concentrated in just a few people's hands.

**opposition** A political group that is opposed to the group in power

**parliament** A group of people who have the duty and power to make the laws of a country

**propaganda** Ideas that an individual or group spreads to influence the thinking of other people

**prosecutors** People in a court who conduct the case against the person who is accused of a crime

**rebellion** An armed fight against the government

**re-education camp** A prison camp designed to change a person's thinking through punishment, torture, hard work, and poor food

**reforms** Changes for the better

**revolution** The overthrow of a government to set up a new or different system of government

**secret police** A police organization that operates secretly for the political purposes of its government

**separation of powers** A political system of keeping the executive, legislative, and judicial branches apart so they do not influence each other

**Soviet Union** Also known as the Union of Soviet Socialist Republics, a country formed of 15 now-independent republics

**term limit** A legal check on the number of times a person can serve in same political office

**totalitarian** Relating to a political system that requires its citizens to blindly follow the rules of the government and that controls all aspects of life, including politics, economy, culture, religion, and the private lives of citizens

**veto** The power of a ruler to stop the passage of an act that has been approved by a legislature

**whim** A sudden idea or wish to do something

**World War II** A war fought from 1939 to 1945 in which the United Kingdom, the United States, France, Russia, China, and other countries defeated Germany, Italy, and Japan

# FOR MORE INFORMATION

## Books

Fandel, Jennifer. *Dictatorship*, Forms of Government. Mankato, MN: Creative Education, 2007.

Haugen, Brenda. *Adolf Hitler: Dictator of Germany*, Signature Lives. North Mankato, MN: Compass Point Books, 2006.

Haugen, Brenda. *Joseph Stalin: Dictator of the Soviet Union*, Signature Lives. North Mankato, MN: Compass Point Books, 2006.

McCarthy, Rose. *Dictatorship: A Primary Source Analysis*, Primary Sources of Political Systems. New York: Rosen Publishing Group, 2004.

Tames, Richard. *Dictatorship*, Political and Economic Systems. Chicago: Heinemann Library, 2008.

## Websites

Academic Kids: academickids.com/encyclopedia/index.php/Dictatorship

How Dictators Work: people.howstuffworks.com/dictator.htm

Famous Dictators: www.biography.com/people/groups/political-leaders/dictators

# Index